Can't Read

Can't Write

D1503712

Here's My Book.

Michael
Jacques

Can't Read, Can't Write, Here's My Book.
By Michael Jacques
Edited by Meghan Greeley

www.heresmybook.com

Book design by Kaila Jacques & Chris Lynn

Illustrations in order of appearance by:
Kaila Jacques, Flavia López, Raylene Knutson,
Mariana Nemer, Katherine Ross, Ben Lory,
Adrian Forrow, Tristan Marantos, Odran McAtamney,
and Chris Lynn

Printed in Canada by FLASH Reproductions

ISBN: 978-1-7753550-0-7
Library and Archives Canada

**A book for anyone who
has been told they can't...**

You
Can.

Foreword

By Marcel (Father)

Can't Read, Can't Write, Here's My Book—interesting title, and hopefully one that will cause you to stop, think, and perhaps read. This book was written—well, not actually written, per se—with the help of speech-to-text technology. It was dictated to an iPad by my son Michael, who has an intellectual disability and autism. This is an invisible disability; others who do not know Michael will see him as "normal."

This story is not a sad one. It is optimistic and positive, and will hopefully inspire others who are travelling the same journey as Michael, or perhaps others who will meet individuals like Michael throughout their lives. To be clear, there are times when life is not fair and times when Michael has struggled. But with hard work and a positive attitude, he has been able to overcome most obstacles in his life.

Being the parent of a child with a disability can be very difficult at times. I've questioned why I was chosen to be blessed—yes, blessed—with a child as unique as my son. Initially, when professionals told us that Michael had deficits, we naturally started thinking of all the things he could not or would not do! It certainly was difficult, but with time, I realized that Michael had so many positive characteristics and skills that we/he needed to tap into in order to live a very productive and positive life. If you are a parent who has recently been told that your child has a disability, try not to be overwhelmed with all the negative thoughts you may have. Try to focus instead on all the positive things that your child can and will do as they grow older—with, of course, the support of you and your community.

Over the last several years, Michael had a vision to write a book. He can now proudly say that he has.

By Debbie (Mother)

Where do I begin when I think of my son Michael? I definitely know I could write forever about how much he has accomplished and how much I have learned from him. His smile and his giggles, which I hear throughout my day, warm my heart. He has touched so many lives and will continue to touch many more. Countless people have come up to me and asked, "Is this your son?" When I say yes, they tell me, "We have never met a person as kind as he is." I respond as a proud mom: "I know."

Michael has changed our lives, and he has grown and matured to be an amazing young man. He has done so much to make this world a better place. To quote his words, so appropriately used in one of his videos: "Every day I feel human because I work and I belong." It's a simple but powerful sentiment, one that we tend to forget in our busy lives. Michael, I am in awe of you, and I know that you are the best version of yourself. You will continue to make a difference.

By Kaila (Sister)

Michael has written a book to prove that strengths and abilities will always surpass any challenges you may be presented with throughout your life. Like anyone, Michael has goals and aspirations; he has worked very hard and surrounded himself with support to become the man he is today. Michael lives every day with a positive outlook, and a kind and compassionate heart. The greatest gifts Michael has given me, his older sister, is the gifts of understanding, empathy, and acceptance. This book offers many lessons and insights through the lens of my brother's journey. Our hope is that this book reaches a global audience and inspires many to look at what we all CAN do. We should embrace and celebrate our differences, learn from one another, and ask ourselves what we can offer. I hope that my brother's story encourages you to look beyond the label of a 'disability' and focus solely on abilities; I hope that it makes you question the idea of 'normal' and why we've set this measure in life. Michael is an honest individual who is wise beyond his years, and I hope that his determination to create positive change will inspire you to do the same.

Acknowledgments

First, I'd like to thank all the people that helped make my book. I'd like to thank my sister Kaila and her husband Chris; without them I would not have been able to produce my book for the world. I would like to thank the people who did the drawings throughout the book; this helped me be able to read it. I'd like to thank Meghan, who looked over my book and made sure my voice was there. I know this is a bit strange, but I'd also like to thank my iPad for allowing me to make my book in a different way. And a big thank you to my parents, whose support I really appreciate. They always push me to achieve my dreams.

Now I'd like to thank all the people who have been a part of my life over the years. You've given me the stories to tell others and made me the person I am today. Thank you to the staff from St. Alexander Catholic Elementary School and all the staff from Notre Dame College School who helped me while I was a student. Thank you to Sobeys for giving me an opportunity to get a job and to the staff that helps me grow everyday. Thank you to Community Living Ontario's program Re:Action4Inclusion for helping me to find my voice and to Community Living for allowing me to advocate for others. Lastly, I'd like to thank everyone who has supported me in my life, because without them I would not be the person I am today. Hopefully I didn't forget anyone!

ILLUSTRATION BY KAILA JACQUES

Writing
My Book

Hi, my name is Michael.

I am twenty-six years old and I live in the Niagara Region of Ontario, Canada. I was born on October 5th, 1991. At the time, no one knew that I was a very special child.

When I was two years old, my parents realized that my behaviour was not correct for my age. My speech was delayed and I had a hard time doing things that other people my age were doing. I was also very awkward. This was the beginning of numerous visits to many different healthcare professionals. I was in grade one when I was diagnosed with Pervasive Developmental Disorder-Not Otherwise Specified (PDD-NOS).

PDD-NOS is a form of autism. There are lots of types of autism, and PDD-NOS falls near Asperger's on the autism spectrum. When I was old enough to understand more about my diagnosis, I was confused because PDD-NOS and Asperger's seemed the same to me, but my parents explained that PDD-NOS was my diagnosis. It was also determined that I had an intellectual disability.

My parents always described disabilities as "challenges." They thought that this word was less negative. I agree, and you'll see that I use that word, too. A disability doesn't mean you *can't* achieve something; it just means that certain things might be a little more challenging.

I would like to say that not all people who have challenges are the same. I'll give you an example: I've met other people with my diagnosis and yes, we have similarities, but in other ways we are completely different. For example, my reading level is very primary, about a grade one level, but some people who have the exact same disabilities as me can read at a higher level. People can have different disabilities or the same disabilities, but everyone is different in their own way.

It might surprise you, now that you know about my low reading level, to be reading my book. It might surprise you even more if I told you that I can't write, either! But I decided that I should tell my life story so that other people with my disability, or anybody who doesn't think

I say "exactly" a lot and Siri would say "Zac Lee."

that they can do something, could hopefully get something out of it. That would mean a lot to me. But also I am doing this for myself; I can't read or write, but making this book can prove to myself— and to everybody else—that even though a person may have some difficulties, it doesn't mean they can't achieve what they set out to do. Sometimes it might take a long time, but that's OK. I started writing this when I was twenty-one, and I'm finishing now when I'm twenty-six.

At first I wasn't too sure how to write my book, and I could not have done it without using my iPad's speech-to-text function. My dad first introduced me to this technology so that I could use Facebook, because I didn't want to be left out. It's been a helpful tool for me. So when I decided to write my book, I knew just the person to help me: Siri!

Whenever I wanted to work on my book, I'd get my iPad and start talking to Siri. Some-times I'd have to take breaks and watch Netflix. I'd always work alone in my room or in the family room. I should tell you that I can never sit still, so whenever I speak to the iPad, I'm always walking around and pacing. This gets the juices flowing and helps me find my ideas. If I spent a couple of days not working on the book, I'd have to listen to where I left off and then I'd start writing again.

Siri doesn't always understand what I'm saying, and speech-to-text sometimes has glitches. My words often don't come out clearly.

For example, I say "exactly" a lot, and Siri interprets that as "Zac Lee"—and I definitely don't know a Zac Lee. But that's why I got some help from a friend. Her name is Meghan. She is very nice and she worked with me to edit my book. Meghan helped me to correct the mistakes.

I spent a lot of time writing, but I didn't really tell anyone what I was working on. One year, while my sister was home for Christmas, she noticed on my iPad that I was writing a book. She was very impressed and asked me lots of questions. She wanted to help, so we went to her studio in Toronto and there we used a whiteboard to write down all the things I could talk about. After this we went to Dairy Queen and I ate so much that I was full for the rest of the night—and I *never* get full. Kaila emailed me all the things I had to talk about, and I slowly worked to finish all the chapters.

Lots of people worked on this book with me. You'll learn more about some of them because they're my friends and family. Other people helped me as well, and I guess you could say that they're my friends now, too. Sometimes I couldn't remember everything that happened to me, so my parents helped me with memories from when I was little. But most of the book is me.

I should tell you a bit about why my book looks this way. My sister and I decided to use larger text; this was to make the book accessible, but also to fill in more pages. I wanted a thick book. The little pictures throughout the text help me to follow along. I can't read, but I can remember each story I wrote by looking at the pictures. Also, when we decided to have chapters that relate to topics, we decided to ask ten illustrators to draw divider pages for specific chapters. This helps me know what the chapter is about, and the different "looks" help me to remember. The illustrators each read a chapter and then were inspired to draw something. They would show me concepts and sketches, and I would give them some feedback. For example, the "Independence" chapter is about me working at Sobeys, and for my uniform, I can't wear colourful running shoes. They have to be black. But the illustrator didn't know that; he was being creative. My sister told me that I don't have to follow the dress code in my book. And I'm OK with that.

You'll notice a lot of green throughout the book. I chose it because it's my favourite colour. I also like orange, because I'm really into Harley-Davidson Motorcycles. Chris and my sister took me to a bookstore to show me covers of other books. I liked covers with big type because it is bold and catches your attention. I also think that the title of my book is catchy and I want it to be what people read first. We include large quotes in the book to emphasize important things I say. The process of making this book was very rewarding.

Childhood

Diagnosis

When I was young, my mom and dad noticed that I did not crawl, talk, or walk by the time I should have. They took me to doctors to find out what was going on. I started participating in swimming and gym at Brock University, which was meant to help me develop my motor skills. My parents tell me that when I got older, I liked to walk on my

tippy-toes. They have pictures and videos of me doing this. They used to call me the "little ballerina." They thought it was cute, but they knew that other children did not behave like that. Also, when I got excited—especially during the holidays—I would flap my hands up and down really fast. To tell you the truth, at twenty-six years old, I still do this in private. This is one of my autism traits; it is a stimulator, and I do it when I'm excited.

When I started speaking, my parents could understand me because they were around me all the time. But when my aunt came over, she noticed that my speech was not clear and that I was very difficult to understand. When I was approximately three years old, my mom and her sister took me to a doctor at McMaster University. The doctor said that it would be a good idea to put me in speech therapy. I remember that when I was young, the therapist used to put shaving lotion on a mirror and I would use my finger to try to spell words. This is a sensory activity, and they tried different modes of learning with me, like hearing, seeing, and feeling. Not sure it worked, but it was fun!

Many doctors also recommended therapies to help me with my walking and balance. They said that I was big for my age, and thought that this might be the reason for my awkwardness.

When I was finally diagnosed in grade one, my mom told me that she cried, but that was the last time she did, because she knew that I would be amazing. These words were said many times throughout my life.

Play

I had many toys when I was younger, but I did not want to play with them; I preferred to play with string instead. My parents tell a story about how I loved to get the ropes from my dad's housecoats and tie them all together. I would then hang this down over the staircase as if I was fishing, even though there was nothing to catch below. When I think about this now or talk to my parents about it, I realize that these behaviours were a part of my disability.

Lots of times I decided to play alone because it was easier for me to do things by myself; that way I didn't have to explain what I was doing.

CHILDHOOD

When I was diagnosed in grade one, my mom told me she cried, but that was the last time she did, because she knew I would be amazing.

My mom told me that when I was at school, I would sometimes leave circle time and go stare outside or play with the string on the blinds. Today I still like to be alone from time to time, especially to relax and watch Netflix and the Movie Network. But most of the time I like doing things with people because I've become a lot more social.

I have been told that I was very clumsy. One day I was playing baseball in the backyard with my sister and our babysitter, and I was the back catcher. I was too close to my sister when she swung, and I got hit in the face with the bat and my two front teeth came out. There were many other times that proved I was a clumsy child. For example, when I was three years old, I tripped over my own two feet and my teeth hit the coffee table. My top four front teeth were pushed back up into my gums. I'm still clumsy to this day, but I walk fine and everything. I should mention that I'm 6'4"—maybe that has something to do with it? Who knows!

When I was young, I also didn't always understand what I was told. For instance, one time I wanted to go on a toy car ride outside of a department store. My mom had told me to wait and that she would give me money for the ride after she went shopping. However, I did not wait, and when my mom turned around, I was not there. When she finally found me I was already sitting on the ride, waiting for my mom to put money in the slot.

3

ILLUSTRATION BY RAYLENE KNUTSON

Family

Parents

 I want to talk to about my parents. My mom's name is Debbie and my dad's name is Marcel. I think it's important that I tell you about their education. My mom graduated with a Child and Youth Worker diploma from St. Lawrence College in Kingston, Ontario. My dad went to university and graduated with numerous degrees. Eventually he became a teacher and went on to get a master's degree in Special Education. My dad must've liked school because he never left— he was a principal and is now retired. My mom is currently working in a high school, where she helps individuals who have social, emotional, or behavioural issues.

My parents had some experience with the ins and outs of the school system because they were working within it, and so they were able to help me out. I know that some parents don't have that kind of experience, so that is why this is an important thing to talk about. Hopefully everybody with a disability (or even no disability) is fortunate enough to have the same support that I have had. Everyone needs parents who listen and ask lots of questions, who speak up for their children and let them find their voices.

Today I live with my parents and they give me rides to work, take me to my meetings, wake me up if I sleep in, drive me to see my friends, and pretty much do everything for me that I need.

FAMILY

Sister

I have an amazing older sister named Kaila. She helps me out with everything. For example, when I was twenty-two years old, she made baseball cards for my Special Olympics baseball team, just like the trading cards for the major leagues. More recently I had an idea for creating my own T-shirts and accessories, and she made the design for me because she's a graphic designer. She also helped me choose the T-shirt fabric because there are certain kinds I don't like. She made my business cards and PowerPoint presentations for my public speaking engage-ments, as well as a video for when I was giving a presentation once on Family Day. My presentation was all about family, so it's pretty cool that someone from my family made a video for me. In the video, Kaila talked about how having a brother like me made her a better person and that she learns a lot from me. Kaila works for one of the top design companies in Toronto, but she still makes time to help me with the things I need to do, and it means a lot.

My sister did her master's thesis paper on me. Or maybe it was about individuals like me, but I know she mentioned me a lot. She made an app for people who have challenges similar to mine, like reading and writing, general organization, and some other challenges like that. She also did a PowerPoint presentation—

FAMILY

like I said, it was about me, so she showed some pictures and told her life story about both growing up with me and how she helps me and how I help her. I'm very close with my parents and my sister.

Kaila has taken me on a couple of trips for my birthday. I also go to see her in Toronto sometimes. Visiting Kaila was the first time I ever went by myself on the train. My dad drives me to the station in Burlington, and he tells me every time, "Don't fall asleep." I have to sit where the conductor is so I don't miss my stop. My sister meets me at the station in Toronto and then we walk to her house. She just moved, but I can still find my way to her new house, and I really don't need her to come pick me up. The other day I showed her that I knew the way, and she was impressed. This makes me feel more independent —I bet my parents wouldn't even know which way to go.

Kaila's husband, Chris, is also a graphic designer. For school, they made three books about sign language, designed to help people learn to sign. Now Kaila and Chis have helped me create my own book. They worked on the design, and asked a bunch of their friends to help with the illustrations. But I got to make all the final decisions, which was pretty cool.

Grandparents

Now I would like to talk about my grandparents. I was very close to all of them. I never met my grandpa, my mom's dad, because he died when I was two years old. But I hear lots of stories about him and see pictures. A couple of years after he passed away, my grandma came to live with me and my family. She took me to my very first day of school. I did other things with her, too. We enjoyed watching TV together. I would sit with her for hours. Also, sometimes she had to get her hair washed, so I helped my mom do it.

When I was little, I had a kitchen set that I would pretend to wash dishes with, and I used to splash cold water on her head when she was sleeping on the couch for a joke. We shared a good sense of humour. She was also my partner in eating candy; she was the only person who could eat the exact same amount as me, and she also really liked Halloween, just like I did. She used to dress up and go around trying to scare me and my family members for a joke. We did basically the same things for about twenty-plus years, until she died in April 2015.

Now I would like to talk to you about my Pépé and Mémé. They are my dad's parents. I used to go to their house all the time in Windsor, and I used to sit with them outside and have ice cream and sing the national anthem in French, and I learned some words in French, too. We went on different trips with them and went to church on Sundays. We also played a card game called Thirty-One together. We did a lot of things over the years.

My Pépé died when I was sixteen years old and my Mémé recently came to live with us. So I've always had grandparents living with me. Mémé can make pies from scratch and different foods as well. I like all of her cooking. We still play Thirty-One and watch different shows together, like *Jeopardy!* and *Wheel of Fortune*. In the summer time, if I'm not working, I go outside for walks with Mémé and when we come back we have ice cream in a cone or sometimes in a bowl, and we sit outside for a while together.

It is hard for me to talk about my feelings, but when I lost my grandparents, it was sad and kind of frustrating. I thought of everything I did with them, and it felt weird to not be doing those things anymore. But I don't want to be negative or sad. I had great experiences with all my grandparents, and now I have great memories. That's why I got my first tattoo in their honour— I talk about that later in my book—and I wouldn't change it for the world.

Cousins

Two of my cousins have disabilities that are completely different from mine. One of them,

Tabitha, has autism, and she also has had problems with her heart. She is doing really well and she always amazes me. She went to the Special Olympics Provincial Games, like me, and I believe she got three or four gold medals in swimming. She also went to the Special Olympics National Games and I'm very proud of her.

I have another cousin named Christopher. Like I was saying, he is completely different in that he has a rare disability called Wolf-Hirschhorn syndrome. Doctors said that he wouldn't live that long, but he is still alive and doing really well in his own way. I should tell you a bit about him. He doesn't speak and doesn't hear or see well. They thought he would not be able to walk on his own, but now he does. He also needs assistance with everyday things like eating, changing, and things most of us take for granted. He makes lots of sounds and can sign some words. Oh, and he is also a big Maple Leafs fan. I'm definitely very proud of him as well.

The weird thing is, my cousins and I were all born around the exact same year. Tabitha was born in 1990 and Christopher was born in 1991 and I was also born in 1991, so that's another reason why we are close. They have helped me realize my potential. I've watched them grow up to become strong individuals and not let anyone else's opinion stand in their way.

4

ILLUSTRATION BY MARIANA NEMER

Learning

That was the day people learned that I was a person.

Elementary School

When I was four years old I started school. I have a picture of my grandma taking me on my first day. I love this picture; it helps me to remember the caring and loving person that she was.

My parents have often told me that they were nervous about me going to school because they work in schools and certainly know the challenges that students face if you are different. They were always involved in my education and initiated meetings as needed.

I have been told that it was difficult to figure out how to teach me. I was pretty good, though, at repeating information I heard. For instance, one day the Education Assistants (EAs) were talking in front of me, and I told my parents what they said. I think people forget that I am still here when they are having conversations or speaking about me. There was a meeting the next day. That was the day people learned that I was a person.

When I was in grade eight, my parents started taking me to parent/teacher interviews and my Identification Placement Review Committee (IPRC) meetings. They thought it was a good idea to involve me in the conversation; after all, it was my education. If it was necessary for adults to talk first, this would happen and then I was included. Maybe my parents knew (or maybe they didn't realize) that they were teaching me to have a voice. Even in grade eight, I was able to let people know what would or would not work. I didn't always under-stand what they were talking about, but my mom and dad decided that this didn't matter. They knew that one day I would get it and that this was helpful for my development.

Words and reading were not easy. My parents supported my reading challenges in numerous ways. I went to summer school at Brock University to work with a teacher who was taking Special Education courses. My parents also privately hired a retired teacher to help me read. My mom says to this day that she never understood (even though I know she did, deep down) why I didn't know the word "the" and other abstract words from one day to the next. I'm sure my parents were frustrated at times.

I believe that because my parents included me in all those meetings, I was well aware of my struggles and very comfortable in my own skin. I recall the summer before grade nine, in summer school, when the teacher asked me to read a Bible passage in front of approximately sixty students. Instead of leaving out of embarrassment, I simply asked the teacher to pick someone else because I couldn't read.

High School

Let me tell you about the three experiences I had in high school: the Good, the Bad, and the Ugly.

First: the Ugly. One of the most stressful times for my mom and dad was when I started high school. I was going from a small school in which everyone knew me to a new school with over one thousand students. I was very nervous; however, my parents were more worried than I was. They had talked to the school in the beginning and it was arranged that I would not get credits in my classes. They felt that because I was at a grade one level in all subjects, I would not be successful, and they wanted the school to focus on my happiness.

My first two years were difficult. I was in a segregated class for two periods a day for my reading and math delays, but this time seemed like forever. Even though I was in my regular classrooms for the rest of the time, I remember those two classes the most. During those classes I had to focus on the things I couldn't do. They were trying to make it better for me, to see if I could learn more, but it wasn't happening.

One day I had a supply EA, and she noticed that I did not belong in this class. She noticed that the other students were lower functioning and that some were non-verbal. Because I was able to talk and communicate to the teachers, I stood out to her. She saw my potential and she didn't feel that this was the right environment for me. She talked to the teacher and she talked to me. She told me to use my voice. I started to realize that I was more than this, and that there are different ways to learn. I realized that I could focus on my strengths and use my voice to speak up.

I went home and talked to my parents, and they made a meeting for me to talk to the teachers. That's how I got out of segregation. Now I was in the regular classes. These were called locally developed classes—you have university level classes, then college level classes, and then you have the "you're not going to university or college" level classes, and there were very few people in those. I was a little nervous because I thought it would go badly; I still couldn't read, write, or do math that well. But I had lots of support from EAs, my teachers, and peer helpers. I also took fewer classes in a semester. So I was fine. I did pretty well in those classes.

And now for the Bad. The Bad part of high school was when things got more challenging. In grade eleven, a resource teacher talked to me about starting to get credits. I had matured and felt like I could do this. Some people don't always get a high school diploma, but you can try to get a certificate of recognition, which means you just complete fewer credits. I wanted to do this.

However, when I started to receive some credits, I decided to see if I could get all my credits and get a high school diploma— and that's exactly what I did. The supply EA who helped me out in the beginning came back, but by now she was a teacher. She helped me because now some of my classes were harder to do. We came up with an idea: I would take classes more than once. Since I can't read or write, I had to memorize everything, and we decided that repetition might help. So I would take a class, and then the next year I would take the exact same class all over again. At first I felt a little uncomfortable because I had to start some of my grade nine and ten classes from scratch. It was also hard because I was a lot older than the people in my class; in Ontario, people with disabilities are allowed to stay in high school until they are twenty-one.

Working towards getting credits was difficult for me and I needed a lot of breaks; I had to go for walks all the time to relieve the stress I was under. It was hard being at high school for so many years when I didn't have a lot of friends. I had goals, and they were important, but it's harder to achieve your goals when you feel lonely. But during those years I had a resource room all the time, where I could go to get help with my homework and stuff, so that part was OK.

Finally: the Good. In my last year of high school I was supposed to take a literacy test to get my high school diploma, but I couldn't read or write, so I had to take a literacy course instead, which was a full semester long. I passed! Even though the doctors said I would never graduate with a high school diploma, I did. It took me seven years, but I graduated with honours and received an award at Notre Dame College School. Oh yeah, I almost forgot to mention—I graduated just before I turned twenty-one.

Time

I'm not good with time. Sometimes in school, during recess or lunch or on a break from class, I would walk around not knowing what time it was. To me, it always felt like just a couple of minutes had passed, but sometimes I stayed out for longer than that—sometimes even for forty-five minutes or more. I usually got paged over the school speaker to go back to class. When I got an iPod, I starting using it to tell time. This is one of the tools that helped me.

When I was younger, to help with understanding how long something would be, my parents would say I had to "wait one TV show." Then I would always ask them, "...Is it done yet?" I don't think this worked for me because if I turned on the TV and it was halfway through a show, I didn't understand how long I had to wait. The iPod or a digital screen helps me see or know the time, but an actual timer really helps me to do things. At work I use my iPod timer and set it to fifteen minutes, and I can see it count down—when it goes off, I know when to go back to work. This still doesn't mean I know what fifteen minutes feels like.

When I was little I use to get so excited for

special occasions like my birthday, Halloween, and Christmas. I actually still do. I would go to the calendar and count the days, but it was still hard to know how long I had to wait.

Disabilities: Then And Now

In grade ten, my teacher asked me if I would like to go to an event called Re:Action4Inclusion. Re:Action4Inclusion is a program within Community Living Ontario for high school students to gather once a year to discuss ways in which to make inclusion better at their schools. This was done through a weekend-long leadership conference. I said yes, and my teacher went into details about the event. She told me it would take place at the beginning of March and that I would be sleeping over for a couple of nights. She told me that there would be activities such as a campfire and something called "Drum Café," and that there would be public speakers. After that we would talk about what changes we could make in high school to create a more inclusive environment.

There were guest speakers at the event. There was one who stood out from the rest. His name was Norman. He talked about challenges, and what he said made me think. He talked about how people with challenges in the old times would be put into institutions. I did not

LEARNING

It also made me think about how all people are normal and how we should all be treated the same.

know much information about this at the time, but I would soon find out. He talked about the different kinds of institutions that existed through-out Canada, and about how when people with disabilities were born, their parents were given a choice to send them away. He went into detail about what happened in these institutions and he showed us pictures. Norman told us that some countries still do this today, and I thought about my own challenges and about my cousins' challenges, and that scared me. I did not have to worry about this happening to us because we live in Canada.

Norman said that people with disabilities have always been around, even in Biblical times, though they were sometimes killed. This scared me, too. But it also made me think about how all people are normal and how we should all be treated the same. After all, even people who are born without disabilities can sometimes develop them later in life, or experience their own challenges due to accidents. It could happen to anybody.

I learned a lot from Norman. He had challenges, too, and that is why this experience was so cool to me; I realized that if you talk about something, people will listen. I left the event feeling inspired to make changes and be a voice for people, both those with challenges and those without.

5

ILLUSTRATION BY KATHERINE ROSS

Belonging

People didn't understand my challenges, partly because I look normal —whatever that means.

Bullying

Now I would like to talk to you about the stages of bullying. The first one is physical, like pushing and punching and things like that. The second one is mental, like saying words to people to hurt them and make them feel small and bad about themselves. It's kind of like cyber bullying, but in this case there's no computer between them— that's the difference. I wasn't part of any of that, but there was another type of bullying at my school, and it was the third kind: exclusion. This is the kind of bullying that happened to me the most.

I think that sometimes people don't realize what they're doing to others by not including them. For me, this mostly happened in elementary school. For example, I could not keep up with the other boys when they played sports at recess, so they would not let me participate. I understand now that the other kids just didn't know how to include me in games or activities because I was different, but that doesn't make it right. And I definitely didn't understand this at the time.

My mom said it broke her heart that I was not invited to many birthday parties. My parents talked about this with some of the support staff, who didn't understand my challenges, partly because I looked normal—whatever that means— and they would ask me to do work that I did not understand, thinking I was just pretending that I couldn't do it. It was sometimes frustrating that people didn't understand me.

When I was in high school, it was a little bit better, but I still experienced exclusion in different ways. It wasn't always bad, but I want you to understand what it was like for me, and hopefully my story will change people's minds and opinions so they will stop doing these things and be nicer and more understanding of every-body's feelings. A person might not even think that they are doing anything wrong, just like the kids in my elementary school. But exclusion *is bullying*. I want people to know that, so I can help change this for everybody, so none of this stuff exists anymore.

In my high school there were different kinds of friendships. There were lots of people who I would say "hi" to or have a small conversation with, but there were not a lot of friends who I could ask to hang out with or who would ask me to hang out after school. I know that other people have lots of friends and go to parties and people's houses or movies with each other. Typical teenager things. There were lots of times I was not invited, and I'm not sure why. Maybe people didn't know how to ask me, or maybe they thought I'd be a burden because they'd have to look out for me since I needed more assistance in some areas. Or maybe they just didn't like me as a friend like that. That was my whole high school experience, for seven years. There were some people who were nicer, and I did have people come over sometimes and once I got invited to a football game, but stuff like that didn't happen very often.

At recess sometimes I would stay inside in the sensory room, which is a calm space. Sensory rooms can have special lighting, sounds, objects to touch, and certain smells. It's a way to develop your senses. For me it was a safe and relaxing experience. Most of the time, though, I would go outside and walk around and try to talk to people. If that didn't work, I would try and find the teachers to talk to. One of my EAs had a lot of interests similar to mine. He enjoyed music and had a motorcycle, just like my dad, and we got along together well. We also had a similar sense of humour. He would take me to his house and we would make pizza or homemade bread. He would take me to movies and dinner. I would spend time with his kids, playing video games or going swimming in his pool. He was a good adult friend for me to have.

Also, if you have certain challenges, funding through the provincial government provides you with a support worker who will hang out with you and help you develop social skills. They do different things with you, like take you to movies and hockey games, and I had a couple of these

BELONGING

workers. This was fun for me because it was outings that weren't with my parents, and it was typical teenage things that I would want to do.

Some advice I would give is to try expand your circle of friends. There are all types of people in high school: football players, cheer-leaders, nerds, people with disabilities... It isn't great to consider labels like this, but usually there are these cliques and this separation of groups, even popular people vs. unpopular people. I would just say that everybody has their own strengths and wants to be included and happy. Acknowledge everyone and say "hi" to everyone, and be kind and don't leave anyone out. If you notice that someone is being left out, do something about it. This would lead to a better school situation for everybody.

Even as an adult, I sometimes experience negativity. This happens when people have misconceptions about those with challenges. One time, for example, when I was of age to drink, someone came up to me and asked if I was all right to be drinking when I have a disability. "Does it affect anything?" they asked. My answer was no. I'm just like everybody else; there are no problems with drinking that I am aware of.

Now that I'm older, I'm able to look back on the bullying that I faced and understand it a little better. Learning to understand has made me the person I am today. So you know what? Enough talking about all the negatives. Overall, I had great support and guidance over the years, and I couldn't be more grateful for this.

Friendship

In senior kindergarten, my family moved from Burlington to the Niagara Region. Our new next-door neighbours had a child who was one year younger than me. His name was Daniel. We both liked video games and we played together a lot. My mom made a rule that we had to switch turns after dying four times. But I wasn't as good as Daniel, so I would die real quick and Daniel would finish the whole freaking game while I watched. I guess that wasn't a very good rule, but it worked out for Dan.

Shortly after we moved into our new house, school started up again. I was very nervous; the only friend I had was Daniel, and he would not be attending my new school. This made it very difficult, because it meant that I had to work hard to make new friends.

I really do not remember much, but over the years I have talked to my parents about my experiences making friends. I do remember that I got along better with the girls; it seemed that boys had a harder time including me because of my differences. But Daniel wasn't like the others.

He became my best friend, and now, many years later, we are still very close—almost like brothers. In fact, when Daniel got married, he asked me to play a very important role in the wedding.

At first Daniel wanted me to be one of his groomsmen, and I said that I would be honoured. I did not yet know who would be the best man. One day we went to a park with some of his friends to play a game of frisbee. I was not very good at it. Daniel and I were a team, and he joked with me, saying, "My best man better be good at frisbee because I don't want him to make me look bad." I said to Daniel, "I really suck at frisbee. I know this." Daniel said, "Michael, you're not understanding me. I asked you to be my best man!"

I was very happy—this meant a lot to me. We started to plan stuff, and Daniel asked some of the groomsmen to share my responsibilities, probably because I can't do certain things. They were his roommates and knew me, and they said that of course they would help.

We had two bachelor parties. One was at his dorm, and we just had beers and pizza and played video games and some board games. It was a very fun time. Then we had another bachelor party in Hamilton, Ontario, and we played bubble soccer—that was really fun. We also went out for dinner. Then there was a game called Fanny-pack. This is a game where you put words in a fannypack and then the bachelor has to do what it says. We also turned some video games into drinking games. That was a little bit dangerous because we would have to chug a whole beer. We also each had a cigar, and that was not good. I was sick for the very first time from all the smoke.

A couple of months later, the big day arrived. It was time for my best man speech—and it was a little bit different than any other speech at a wedding.

When I was preparing for this I focused on some of my strengths, which, as I said, don't include reading and writing. So my sister and her husband helped me make a video of me doing my speech in advance, so I could play it at the wedding. I had to work on what I had to say and memorize it. It was very hard for me to grasp some of the words and act with expression, but this way I didn't have to feel stressed on the big day. I got my tux early and wore it in the video, but since you could only see me from the waist up, I wore my pajama bottoms underneath. While we were filming in the house, somebody came to the door. I probably looked pretty ridiculous answering the door with half the suit on and pajamas on my lower half.

I should tell you how my sister and her husband made the video with me. I memorized some of my speech, but it was too hard when the camera was in front of me to remember all the

Daniel and I both know that true friendship is not about focusing on what people cannot do, but instead focusing on the things we're good at and the things we like.

words in order. I wanted to do a good job and not forget anything. So Kaila would read a sentence and I would repeat it. We filmed the whole thing like this and then Kaila and Chris pieced it together on the computer.

Even though I had the video to show, I still wanted to get up and speak at the wedding, just to say a few words in person. I was really nervous. But when the time came, I went up to the podium and just said a few things before the video started. It all worked out really well. I had found a clip of Daniel in high school dancing to Beyoncé's "Single Ladies," which is a song all about "putting a ring on it," so I included that in my speech video. That was a surprise for Daniel—he probably had no idea how I found that. Everything came together and everybody was happy with my speech. I got a standing ovation and the video was a hit. They played the song a couple more times throughout the night just to bug Daniel, and he was a pretty good sport about it, obviously. Overall, being a part of the wedding was a great experience. And even though I had to do my speech differently than other people might, Daniel and I both know that true friendship is not about focusing on what people cannot do, but instead focusing on the things we're good at and the things we like.

My Grandma taking me to my very first day of school.

My family at Christmas. I'm holding a gingerbread house I made.

This is my Pépé and Mémé.

This is me with my grandma, cousins, and sister. Christopher, who I mention in the book, is in the wheelchair.

This is Dan and me getting ready for his wedding. I was his best man.

I made it! My graduation day.

Community

Sports

When I first started playing sports in school, I played on the "regular" teams. One of these sports was basketball, and that was often a struggle; my skills, focus, and coordination weren't like everyone else's. It was very hard for me to concentrate on where the ball was. I guess it was not fair for everybody. I don't remember this, but my parents told me that some kids on my basketball team were getting mad because I wasn't paying attention when I was on the basketball court—usually I was in la-la land, and I was never where I was supposed to be, like underneath the net or shooting or dribbling up the court. I was not focused, and I also did not run up and down the court fast enough; I was still very clumsy, probably because of how tall I was, and I didn't like running much anyway. It's hard to feel good about something when you don't have the same capabilities as the people around you.

One time my coach tried to see if they could have an extra player on the court—there are supposed to be five players, but because I was not doing much anyway, he just thought that it would make me feel like I was a part of the team and be fairer to the other players. This didn't work out because it was frustrating for me and frustrating for others.

I also played soccer and baseball on the

"regular" teams. I remember being on the exact same team as my friend Daniel for a little while, but since I didn't like running, I was not as fast as other people and the coaches tried to find different ways to keep me on the team. But it just was not working out.

I stopped playing sports for a while. When I was thirteen, my parents encouraged me to get back into it; I think they wanted me to be more social and hang around more with people who have similar skill levels as me. They also wanted me to find something I was good at. So I started participating in the Special Olympics. I wasn't too sure what sports I wanted to do because there are lots of different sports for winter and summer, so I decided to try some out.

First I went bowling. I was not very good at it because my hand was diagonal whenever I threw the ball, and it went into the gutter almost every time. Also, because of my height, I kind of chucked the ball when you're supposed to roll it. I didn't know my own strength sometimes, either. Bowling didn't really work out for me.

Next I tried basketball. I was pretty good at it, and even though I still did not like running, this was much more my speed because my teammates were at a similar skill level. And I had my height advantage, so I could stand under the net and put my arms up and get all the rebounds. So I stuck with it. Then I went to baseball. I liked baseball the best because I was good at it, and there is still some running but not as much, so I had lots of fun. I also tried track and field because I knew by now that I was good at throwing. I liked shot-put, but also had to do a track event and that was too much running for my liking. So I decided to stick with the two sports I liked best.

With basketball and baseball, every couple of years you have a chance to go the Special Olympics Provincial Games. It's exactly the same as the regular Olympics; there are medals, a torch, and big opening and closing ceremonies. It's held in a big arena, and there are people from different regions all around the province.

I've competed in the Special Olympics twice for basketball. I only got a medal once, though, and it was a bronze. But I was still happy. It was lots of fun there. Buses drive you to the events, and there are lots of cops and medics there— the cops even run with the torch at the opening ceremony. Lots of famous people attend. Everybody comes out to watch you, and there are also cameras that film the events for TV. It's only on select channels and not every event is aired, but it's very exciting. There's a dance after the closing ceremony, and I like that sort of thing because I get to talk to people.

If you win a gold medal in one of your sports (or in many different sports) you can go to the

Special Olympics National Games. It's pretty cool. I never got a chance to go that far yet; I had an opportunity once, but it didn't pan out. I know a couple of people who have competed there, and they told me it was awesome.

I'd really like to go to the National Games for baseball someday. I am working on getting better at the different positions. I play second and third base, and I've also been a back catcher and outfielder. I'm a pretty good batter, too—when I hit the ball, it goes far. I can hit it to both sides of the field, and one time I was even nominated for a Most Valuable Player award. I just got a hat and a bag, but it meant a lot to me. Once I also got an unassisted double play! I was on second base and I caught the ball in the air, and then I touched the base and I got one of the opposing players out. It was a great feeling. So who knows—maybe someday you will see me making similar plays at the National Games!

Achievements

I would like to say that my community is very small, but I like it. It's very close, and even though it's small, I think people know me from my job at Sobeys, because I help them out as much as I can there. I'm involved in other community events, too, and people know me from school or from being

All you have to do is believe in yourself and not be afraid to ask for help when you need it, and hopefully we all have people who believe in us.

in the newspaper for Re:Action4Inclusion or for public speaking. Because of my leadership skills in high school, the school board took a picture of me to use for Special Education pamphlets and brochures. They even put a picture of me on a van! I still see the van driving around to this day.

I was nominated for the Ruby Award in 2011, which is given out by the city of Welland/Pelham. The award recognizes people who are leaders and volunteers in the community and who try to help out the people around them. I believe there were ten recipients selected. There were eight from my school, and I was one of them. One of my friends won the award, so I was happy for them. And I was happy to be one of the ten people nominated. There was an event for the Ruby Award and I had to wear a suit and everything. It was a very fun night and I got plaque out of the deal.

In 2013, I received an award from Community Living Welland/Pelham. The award recognizes an individual's efforts in the community or at work to make everybody belong. The recipient is named an Ambassador Of Inclusion. This awards ceremony was fun as well, and I had to give a little presentation. Even though I would always try to include everyone, it was nice to be recognized for it. I was even in the paper; they printed a picture of me and Daniel. There is also a video on YouTube of me getting the award and doing my presentation.

It meant a lot to me to receive this award. I believe that everybody should have the chance, and the right, to do anything they want that will contribute to their community.

Support

Now I would like to tell you about all the people who helped me over the years, and how that support made me the person I am today. Like I said before, my parents, my sister, my cousins, and my grandparents have all helped me, and I'm lucky to have so much support in my own family. But I received help from others as well: my teachers, my EAs, principals, student helpers, Daniel, my friends, my mom's best friend Lori, and (when I got older) my boss and my co-workers. They have all played an important role in helping me find my voice and my independence. So have different organizations or programs, like Community Living, Re:Action4Inclusion, Special Olympics, public speaking, and community involvement—these are all things that helped me to be myself and to never give up, and showed me that anything is possible. All you have to do is believe in yourself and not be afraid to ask for help when you need it, and hopefully we all have people who believe in us. Sometimes we might not be sure who those people are, or whether there are many or few, but there are always people who believe in those around them.

These people have all played some part in my life, big or small, and it made a lasting impression on me and I wouldn't be the same without them.

Independence

ILLUSTRATION BY ADRIAN FORROW

Getting My License

Now I would like to tell you how I got my G1, which is a beginner's level driver's license in Ontario. You're probably thinking to yourself, how can a person with a disability get his G1 when he cannot read or write?

It took a full semester. I worked hard to memorize what my teachers and peer helpers said as they went through the book with me each day. They also helped with the computer test and read the questions aloud to me. I did the G1 practice test online over and over again. Repetition is always helpful for me. We did this for one whole class per day, and sometimes it was a lot to handle, so I had to go for walks to keep from getting too stressed. But then we would get right back to it.

One day I felt ready. I talked to my parents and they looked for a license bureau around my area, and there was one in St. Catharines. Once every month at the license bureau there is a staff member who reads the multiple choice questions to you, and all you have to do is check off or circle the multiple choice answers: A, B, C, or D. There were only a couple of people in the class besides me. I passed on the very first try! I was very happy and surprised, and my parents were happy for me as well. So I had my license for a little while before I went to Apex driving class. Apex helps you to understand driving more, and also helps you get a lower insurance rate. The class is in two parts: the in-class sessions and then the driving sessions.

The first time we went there were lots of people in the class and only one teacher. My parents and I decided that I wouldn't sign up this time around; we went and got more information, and then I went to Apex again in a different time slot, when there were fewer people. I passed the in-class part with an 85% and I was happy with that, and my parents were, too.

Then I moved on to the driving portion. At first I was very nervous, just like any first time driver. It helped that my driver was confident and helped me out in many different areas. In the beginning I kept looking at the gauge to see how fast I was going, so I had to learn how to feel the speed instead. My instructor told me to not press the gas too much or I would go too fast.

At first we stayed in parking lots to learn my right and left turns. We didn't always go on the busy streets; we would stay on the quieter streets so I was comfortable. I became good at depth perception and judging how far or how close things were, because my teacher helped me learn techniques for all that. Turns out I was OK at parallel parking, and overall was pretty OK at driving, too. But I made some mistakes, just like everybody, so I had to continue to work on certain

I wanted to feel freedom and not rely on everyone and have some independence.

things. There was only a set amount of driving sessions included in the course—I think it was ten—so I had to go and see if I could get more lessons. I did, so I was able to practice more. My driver said that I was almost ready for my G2 driving test, but that I still needed more practice.

Eventually my G1 license ran out because it expires after five years, so at some point I'll have to do it again. Even though I didn't get my full license, it was important that I tried. I wanted to feel freedom and not rely on others and have some independence. And this was another accomplishment I can say I made. I know I'll be ready next time, and hopefully I'll do better and get my full license.

Work

In 2007 I did a high school co-op placement. The co-op program gave students an opportunity to work in a hands-on environment. I liked it because it gave me a break from school, and I got to meet new people and work on my social skills. First I did mechanics, and people thought I was good at that because of how friendly I am. My next placement was at the Sobeys in Welland, which was very practical because I learned all about working in a grocery store. When it was over, I decided to apply for a job interview at the Sobeys closer to my house in Fonthill. My mom went and talked to the manager, Ron, to see if I could apply. I had a job interview. I told Ron my responsibilities at the other Sobeys store and I got the job!

 I started working there four days a week—Thursday, Friday, Saturday and Sunday—collecting buggies and helping in the produce section. Now I work Monday through Friday, and sometimes the weekend if I get called in. Everyone there is friendly, and my co-workers help me anytime I need it.

Working at Sobeys is great, especially because in the beginning, they really worked with me to grow. For example, they helped me out with some tools and showed me some tricks. When I first went into produce, there were some jobs that involved reading and a little bit of writing. I also had to figure out the bunkers. These are the shelves where produce is stored, and you had to check the temperature to see if it was cold enough for the vegetables and juices. They gave me a list and a temperature gun, and they marked the bunkers with numbers so that I could follow along. If I had any questions, everybody would help me out in one way or another and I wasn't afraid to ask.

 In produce, you had to know the seven must-haves—that is, the seven kinds of vegetables and fruits you need to have in the store at all times. They are: bananas, red and green grapes, English cucumbers, vine tomatoes, red and green peppers, strawberries, and raspberries. The person who was training me helped me out a lot. He became a real friend. He read me the seven must-haves and I memorized all of them.

In the front of the store there are plants, different kinds of dirt, and firewood that I have to carry out to cars. This involves reading the dirt bags as there are a lot of different types of dirt, and I have to make sure I get what the customer needs. Someone talked to the boss to ask how I could do carry-outs if I can't read, so they figured out a way to make this possible. My co-workers colour-coded the product codes and the bags so I would know which dirt to bring out to the car. A lot of times I would also just ask the customer, "Is it this one?" If they said no, I would ask again until I got the right bag. Because I am a quick learner and because I have a good work ethic, I do more and more things now. Ron showed me different departments that I can help out in and that's what I'm doing now.

I've worked at Sobeys since 2010, and I'll work there until they don't need me anymore, and that's not gonna happen anytime soon. Today I have lots of responsibilities at my job. I help students with their co-op placements, and most of them get jobs at Sobeys afterwards. I have many duties around the store, and the only areas where I don't work are meat department, hot and

It means a lot to have a real job because it makes me an active member of society. It makes you kinda more human, too.

cold deli, seafood, salad bar, cash, and bakery. But I do everything else, including special projects like putting decorations on the Christmas tree, decorating the store, and putting up signs. Just no cash and no knives.

My job does not feel like a job; it feels like a family. Everybody at Sobeys is great. My boss, Ron, doesn't treat me any differently because I have disabilities. He expects lots from me because he knows I can do it, and everybody else follows his lead. I believe everybody respects me and treats me like an equal there.

There is a video of me on YouTube talking about my work at Sobeys and how belonging to a community through a workplace is important. It was done through an organization called People First of Canada. It's an organization for people in the community with disabilities who want to make a difference and become advocates. There were a couple of segments on work and transportation and housing and marriage. I am not too sure if I'm leaving anything out—hopefully not.

It means a lot to have a real job because it makes me an active member of society. It makes you kinda more human, too. I have my own bills and taxes to pay, and I'm always helping people. I'm a talkative and outgoing person—that's just my personality, to be helpful and make sure everyone is happy. Every day I wake up is a good day for me, just because I'm working.

Advocating

Re:Action4Inclusion

I was impacted in many ways during my first experience at Re:Action4Inclusion. One of the main goals they have for you is to come out of your comfort zone. At the time I was a little shy, because I did not know the people, and I was scared to talk to them because I was different. I didn't want to say anything stupid or wrong. Sometimes I mix up words or have a bit of a speech problem and things don't come out clearly. By the end I was able to not worry about that and I was a lot more comfortable talking. I felt like a new person was born, if that makes sense. They were very nice, and I was included in everything, just as if it did not matter that I had challenges—the point was everyone there belongs. That is what people at Re:Action4Inclusion showed me: they want change, and inclusion teaches us ways to make that possible.

During that weekend, we learned many things that we were able to take back to our schools and put into practice. One of the questions we were asked was, "What is real inclusion?" Lots of people have meetings about inclusion and what they *think* it is, so we learned to communicate what real inclusion is from our standpoint, to see if our definitions match up. Then it's up to the people involved in Re:Action4inclusion to take something back to their high schools and address inclusion if they want to make change.

I talked about my own experiences at this conference; I talked about what meaningful, real inclusion means to me, like always finding a way to help out anybody with challenges (or without challenges, too). For example, if people are playing sports and somebody is not good at something, like running with the ball or catching or whatever the case may be, it's important to still have that person participate. Different rules can be put in place to make it fair for everybody. For example, in baseball, you can give five extra seconds to someone who can't run as fast before throwing the ball to the base, and this gives them a fair chance. After a count of five is up, then they are out like everybody else. You don't want to have people with disabilities always being safe on the base or getting a free pass—they still need rules, but these rules can be altered to make it more inclusive and fair for everyone. Making it fair for everybody is what makes it fun for everybody.

Everyone's different, so everyone has to find their own voice and learn what is right for them, and if something isn't working, there's always another way to do it. Over the years, I've learned that everybody can find a way to be good at something. You'd be very surprised what people can actually do if you get to know them better. A lot of people are very talented in their own ways. I like sports, but everybody has their own thing—drawing, music, doing announcements, photography, art, drama. Those are just some examples, but really, if you're good at something, there's an excellent chance that lots of people are good at it, and it's nice to find other people who share your passions.

I've been involved with Re:Action4Inclusion for a very long time now—since high school—acting as a guest speaker, sitting on panels, or showing other people how to run it. I give my input and help with whatever needs to be done. I'm good with anything they throw at me. (I also try to be modest about my work—I know sometimes it doesn't sound like it!) Sometimes they might want me to lead an activity with a group of people or a workshop. They ask me to give some examples of my life experiences. I've even travelled across the province of Ontario as an ambassador for Re:Action4Inclusion. I talk to people about the little things they can do to make high schools better. Some advice I would have for people is to never discredit yourself and never sell yourself short. Always look for different ways to do things if you can't do it the exact same way as others.

I encourage you to think about what real inclusion means. Now that you've read this chapter, I hope you can see what real inclusion is from somebody else's point of view. Does it match your own ideas? Try to think about this at school or at work—wherever you are—and if you see a problem, do something about it. Everybody can make change. All you have to figure out is what needs changing.

Finding My Voice

I have a distinct memory from Re:Action4Inclusion. We had to split into teams of five and talk about what we can do differently at school to be more inclusive. We also had to present our goals. Groups went up one by one to present their ideas for positive change. What they said stuck with me, and it made me think about what I can do differently.

Norman, the same guest speaker who talked about the history of treatment for people with challenges, helped me out a lot. He had cerebral palsy, and he talked about some of the struggles he had growing up. Some of these were the exact same struggles I had. But nothing stopped him from becoming a public speaker. I decided that I was not going to be shy, and that I would start voicing my opinions. I became more independent and confident in myself, because people were now listening to what I had to say. I was shy before because of my speech; sometimes I would talk and say things wrong. But I realized that it was

ADVOCATING

I was shy before because of my speech; sometimes I would talk and say things wrong. But I realized that it was better to talk than to be silent.

better to talk than to be silent. This led me to be more social and have new opportunities for speaking engagements and all these other things that I'm now doing. Like writing this book.

Norman also told us that when you expect life to be hard, it becomes easy, and when you expect life to be easy, it becomes hard. He showed us videos of people in wheelchairs who were dancing, playing basketball, and doing stunts at skate parks. In one of these videos, a guy did flips off ramps, and he went to an event called Nitro Circus, where he did one of the biggest jumps—he went off the ramp and landed it. This just goes to show that anybody can do anything they want to, and it doesn't matter what you can do physically or mentally. All you have to do is believe.

Leadership

During high school I was involved in basketball. My team was called the Raptors, and it was a special needs basketball team. (I'm 6'4", remember, so basketball seemed like a good fit for me.) After Re:Action4Inclusion, I started to notice that most of the things that "regular" teams did, the Raptors were not a part of. For example, we were excluded from pep rallies, sports banquets (we would get our team awards at the end of the year instead of at the sports banquet like everybody else), and even the students vs. teachers basketball game. So I went and talked to the principal and my basketball coach. I explained that this was unfair and made suggestions. We were then involved in those activities. Slowly, things began to change.

I also wanted to include the Raptors in the yearbook. I had noticed that in past yearbooks, the special needs teams weren't included much, if at all. It was my first time taking a photography class, so I talked to my teacher to see if I could bring my team members into the studio to take their pictures. He said that I should bring another student with me and that we should take the pictures in the gym so that everybody could be in it—me included. In yearbook class, I asked my teacher to give me two pages of the sports section for my Raptors pictures. That's how we became included, just like the other teams.

Another thing I did was help organize a students vs. teachers basketball game for the Raptors. It didn't matter to me if I was a part of it myself, or a part of any event, really; I just wanted it to be fair for everybody, because everybody deserves to have a good experience in high school.

I also talked to my principal and to the teacher who ran student council about having a person with a disability become a part of it. I didn't feel that it was the same to have a person without a disability speaking for us, because they would not know what they were talking about. Everybody needs to have their own voice heard, and this way people with disabilities would see that they were a part of the school, just like everybody else. My friend was one of the first people with a disability to be on the student council.

By the time I left, my high school it was more inclusive. It was pretty inclusive before, but I decided to make it a little better. It was something we all had to work on and hopefully I made an impact to make it an even better school.

 **Community Living**

Because of all my community work and public speaking, I was chosen to become a member of the board for Community Living Welland/Pelham. I sat on the board for roughly two years, and then an opportunity arose: I decided to put my name down to run for a spot on the Community Living Ontario board. So I went and got the form and asked my current board to nominate me for this position. At the annual general meeting I believe there were ten people presenting and only seven spots to be filled on the board. All nominees had to give a speech. I went up in front of five hundred people and I was very nervous to speak. Right away I took the mic off the stand and dropped it. I quickly picked it up and said, "Oops, sorry, but I meant to do that." Everyone laughed and I felt a little calmer.

Oh, and I almost forgot to mention: because we were only given a little bit of time to say things about ourselves, my dad printed out highlights of my achievements on paper and we placed them on the tables before my speech. I practiced my speech with my dad a bunch of times, so I felt pretty ready. I talked about the three most important things to know about me, and then I told everyone that the rest is on the print-out. I believe I did well. Other people who spoke had more years of experience, but we all had valuable experience in different areas.

Afterwards, when the votes were tallied, I was very happy and shocked to win a spot. At one point in life I would never have thought that I could achieve something like that, but it just goes to show you that even when you think you maybe did not do your best, you can still be surprised by the outcome. I know I was!

I was now one of the youngest people on the board, but more importantly, I was able to represent people with disabilities and show others anything is possible. I've been on the board since 2016, and it has led to so many great opportunities.

I'm currently the co-chair of an event called A Million Possibilities Solo Ocean Row. It's a campaign that helps to raise awareness for people with intellectual disabilities, and it is also a fundraiser. All proceeds go to four programs within Community Living. It's called Solo Ocean Row because there is a man, Colin, who is going to row across the Atlantic Ocean to help raise awareness for this cause and for his son, who has intellectual and physical disabilities. (He actually finished during the time I wrote my book!) The reason why it is called A Million Possibilities is that I think it's going to take one million strokes to cross the Atlantic. It is also to recognize that there are a million possibilities out there for everyone. And I truly believe this.

It's been awesome having all of these new experiences and advocating for things I care so much about. I hope to be re-elected as a member of the board for Community Living Ontario and learn more ways to stay involved.

Public Speaking

Lots of people around me encouraged me to become a public speaker. People said that I was a natural. I was speaking out about my own experiences and helping other individuals like myself, and people liked seeing me act as a role model. I'm always nervous when I do speaking engagements because I might forget or mess up what I'm supposed to say, but I also think it's a good thing to get nervous because it shows you are passionate and care about what you are doing. You don't want to be overconfident because then you won't connect to people or you might come across as not caring.

Shortly after the very first Re:Action4Inclusion conference, one of my teachers told me that there was an opportunity for me to go and do a presentation at my school board office, because there was an event coming up. I said, "Sure." It was a presentation to the board and lots of parents of children with disabilities were there. The message was to show that there are lots of opportunities for people with disabilities and I was an example.

I was very nervous; it was my first time public speaking, and I wasn't too sure how I was going to do it. But somehow it worked, thanks to my parents and my teachers and other people who helped me to prepare. I just spoke about my life and what I liked to do. I know you'll probably think, "How could he do it without reading and writing?" Well, I used symbols and pictures for my first presentation, kind of like the ones I have included in this book. This helped me to remember where I was and what I had to talk about. I don't always have enough time to show a PowerPoint, so I practice a lot and memorize the key points I need to talk about, and then I kind of freestyle. I mostly practice with my dad. Lately I've been trying to record my voice so that I can listen to it before my presentation, to know what to talk about. But it hasn't been working because I'm usually thinking too much about the recording and what I have to say right instead of talking to my dad and having a more causal interaction.

When the time came for me to do my speech, my EA and my mom were there, along with my principal. I had basketball after my speech, so I had to go first, and I had to wear my high school uniform. I also wore a tie that had my school colours on it. Later people said that I looked like my dad while I was standing at the podium, I guess with my different stances and stuff. Plus my dad was a principal so he gave a lot of presentations. I don't really remember it much—but I was told I was slamming my cue cards down on the podium when I was done with them. I didn't even notice.

After my presentation was done, there was a question and answer period. Some people asked me questions, though I can't remember them now. When I was leaving with my mom, a parent came up to me and talked to me about some of her son's challenges. She was crying. It meant a lot to me to hear her story, because I really saw the difference in her as I showed her all the

I started speaking in classes about my disability and I told my story, and I tried to show how my experience is different than other people's.

positive things her son could do. Getting this type of response makes me feel like I'm making a difference.

I started speaking in classes about my disability and I told my story, and I tried to show how my experience is different than other people's. I think it helped my classmates to see a different side of me. Then I started speaking at a different high schools and gave multiple presentations at Re:Action4Inclusion. Later I began doing presentations at other agencies, and there came an opportunity for me to go to Brock University and present to people who wanted to go into teaching or become an EA (or something in that field). It was lots of fun. I also went to Humber College to a third-year psychology class to talk to the students and I think they learned a lot.

Hopefully I can do a lot more public speaking in the future. I like doing it, and I enjoy helping people to understand things they're not too sure about yet and let them know it's OK to not have all the answers all the time. I hope to inspire people in the same way that I was inspired when I saw Norman.

9

ILLUSTRATION BY ODRAN MCATAMNEY

Adulthood

Tattoos

Growing up, I always wanted a tattoo. My ideas for what that tattoo would be changed all the time. I constantly bugged my parents about it. I remember that I started to really want one when I was seventeen years old, because people I looked up to had a tattoo—or many—and I also watched all the tattoo shows. I thought to myself, "How cool is that?"

Every time my birthday came around, or any time my parents or my sister or whoever didn't know what to get me for a present, I would smile and say, "How about a tattoo?" The answer was always no. My mom used to say, "Wait until you're eighteen." When I was finally eighteen she said, "Wait until you're twenty." When I was twenty she said, "Wait until you're twenty-two." When I was twenty-two I asked her again, and she told me to wait until I was twenty-five. Eventually my parents started telling me to wait until I was thirty. That's when I realized they just kept changing the age.

So I stopped asking. But then, on my twenty-fourth birthday, they surprised me! I was finally allowed to get my tattoo. I also finally knew what I would get. At that time two of my grandparents had recently passed away, so I was thinking about

getting a cross to remember them by. So my sister went online and looked for good local artists, and she found a place in Burlington with a guy who does great tattoos. He has a cool style and I knew my tattoo would be unique.

The day came and we went to Burlington. I went shopping first, got a doughnut, and then I got my first tattoo. It was an amazing experience. The tattoo artist was really good and I was very excited when my tattoo was done. It really didn't hurt at all because the whole tattoo was done with small dots, not lines. The artist was also excited because my sister told him the story about it being my very first tattoo and how long I had wanted one. He was very happy to help me out. Next year my sister gave me a framed poster that said: "Tattoo + Doughnut = Best day ever," which was something I said that day. I still have this poster in my bedroom.

I'm twenty-six now and I have another tattoo: a shamrock, which connects to my Irish roots. (I also really want to go to Ireland some-day.) This one was a little different; instead of the machine, like they usually use for tattoos, I got a stick-and-poke. There are two different ways you can do it: one is by hand, and the other way is with a hammer-like object, which you tap. My sister's friend, Odette (and she's my friend, too) does stick-and-poke tattoos, and she does it the first way, by hand. She is very good at it and I had a great experience. She explained what was happening in each moment, and she went through each step one-by-one. She is very nice and kind as well, so that always helps for the experience. I'm not saying that all tattoo artists are not like this—they typically are—but I'm just saying she is very good at her job. I've been lucky; my first tattoo artist was very good as well, and he explained things to me in a similar way. They were both good experiences, each in different ways.

Another thing I would like to say about my last tattoo artist: I was very impressed with the clean lines she did, especially because she was working by hand. Everybody who saw my tattoo said the same thing. If anyone wants to try a new experience, I recommend trying this style of tattooing.

Hobbies

Me and my dad like motorcycles. We have lots of Harley-Davidson stuff in our "man cave." I like skulls, so I have lots of skulls, too—not real ones, of course.

I enjoy going to concerts. I went to see AC/DC, Rush, and Guns N' Roses. I also went to see some comedians like Russell Peters and Jeff Dunham (I saw Dunham's show twice). I went to see some magicians as well, like Chris Angel. I recently started going to Comic-Con because my friend Caity got me into it. I met some people at Comic-Con who are famous, like two actors from my favourite show, *Sons of Anarchy*. I took pictures with them and got their autographs, which are now in frames in my man cave.

Caity also got me involved in a Zombie Run. It is pretty cool. What you have to do is run through obstacle courses, and there are people who are dressed up as zombies, and the objective is to steal the flags around everyone's waist. If you get someone's flag, they become a zombie and they lose the race. But if they still have a flag they might be able to win the game—it depends on how many flags they have and who is left in the end. I was a zombie and so was Caity. I did pretty well for my first time. I got some flags—not too sure how many, but a lot more than one—and I was proud of myself.

I also got involved in doing a haunted house with Caity. It's called Haunt Manor. She's an actor there, but sometimes she's allowed to have guests come, so I went with her on the day before Halloween. It was a very fun experience. I scared maybe ten people or more that night.

I also like movies and TV shows and lots of different music. I listen to everything once, and if I like it, I wanna listen to more. For movies I like comedies and action-packed movies or anything with a good story. When it comes to TV shows, I've got a whole bunch of favourites—again, I watch everything once and see if I can get into it. Some of my favourites are *The Good Doctor,*

ADULTHOOD

I enjoy going for long walks with my music, because sometimes I do my thinking when I'm walking, or sometimes it's just to relax.

Vikings, The Big Bang Theory, Little Sheldon, The Blacklist, and *Lucifer.* Oh, and also *Lethal Weapon* and *Sherlock Holmes* stand out for me.

I also enjoy going for long walks with my music, because sometimes I do my thinking when I'm walking, or sometimes it's just to relax. Walking helps me to do whatever, really.

I like trying new experiences when I have an opportunity to do them.

 **Travel**

When I was twenty-five, I travelled with some people from Re:Action4Inclusion to a World Inclusion Conference in Florida. It was very interesting because there were people there from all around the world—Australia, England, and places like that. I believe lots of people with various disabilities were represented at this conference. There was a lot of diversity.

There were group sessions to talk about how to make things more inclusive back in our home countries. We were together at the beginning, but then we broke into smaller groups to get different experiences with different people from other cultures and places. There were opening and closing ceremonies, with speeches and things like that, and they had special technology because of all the different languages being spoken. Sometimes we used headsets,

This opened my eyes to how different some places are compared to Canada. But the goal was to try and make all countries inclusive.

and you could listen to the conversations or speeches in your own language.

I got to meet some people, but I didn't have a chance to meet everybody because there were lots of people there. We also had many events to go to, so we didn't always have a chance to hang out with everybody—we only got to do that a few times. This was partly because of everyone's different sleeping patterns, since people were travelling from different time zones. We had a chance to go to workshops, where people spoke about different things they were doing in the world. This opened my eyes to how different some places are compared to Canada. But the goal was to try and make all countries inclusive. There currently are many different levels of inclusion. Some places still have institutions and segregation and others don't.

I didn't get to go to all of the talks because there were too many at the same time. But I did go to a couple, and they were very interesting. I would do something like that again if the opportunity arises.

Another time I went to a forum in Ottawa. The Prime Minister of Canada wanted to hear from young adults who had disabilities and it was invitational—you had to be invited. My name was put forth by Community Living Ontario and the Canadian Association for Community Living. Other people were chosen by their own organizations to go. There were all kinds of people with disabilities there to share their experiences and help make Canada a more inclusive place, and it was hosted by the Ministry of Sport and Persons with Disabilities. There were breakout sessions so people could compare ideas on how to make our country better. There were times when we all gathered in a big room to watch people give presentations. There was special technology to help people follow along, just like in Florida—people could get headsets to listen in French or English or a couple of different languages, and there were also people there to do sign language.

At this forum there were people who were all different and had different needs. Some people needed support workers with them for assistance and to make sure their voices were heard, and of course we were listening. For me, it didn't really matter if my parents came or not; I'm sure they would probably have helped me out if I forgot to say something, but I also like being independent when I can.

Prime Minister Justin Trudeau was there to ask questions and listen to some of the questions people had. It meant a lot to people that he took time out of his day to come to this event, because I'm sure he had lots of other things to do. I shook his hand, but my mom wished I got a photo with him.

Those were my "work" trips, but I've also travelled just for fun. I've been to Las Vegas twice, and when I was there I went to see some magic shows and comedians, and I also went to see the Grand Canyon and the Hoover Dam. Those were pretty cool places to see, and it was lots of fun.

I've been to Florida other times, too. On the most recent trip, I went to Spring Training for the Blue Jays and I went to see some games in the Blue Jays Stadium, in Dunedin. I've also been to a Yankees game at the Yankee Stadium in Tampa Bay and some Philly games in Clearwater, all of which was part of Spring Training. I even had a Philly cheesesteak, which was very good. Those last two trips were with my dad.

I have also been to Chicago. I saw the "big bean" and there are two walls there that have different faces that change on them. I walked a lot in that city. I had a special Chicago deep-dish pizza, and it was very, very tasty. I was able to go to a Chicago Blackhawks hockey game. This trip was with Kaila and Chris.

I also recently went to Los Angeles with Kaila and Chris. It was pretty awesome there as well. We stayed in Venice Beach, and we went to a lot of beaches even though it wasn't that hot, and I walked up and down the sands. You drive a

lot in L.A., and there are always things to see on the way, but one of my habits in car rides is to nap. I would fall asleep even if it was a ten minute car ride. I saw the Hollywood Sign. We went to some museums and just walked around to different places and ate lots of food. If we saw something we wanted to do, we went and did it.

I've been to other places as well, but I just can't remember them. Hopefully I get to travel to more places with my family, like Ireland, Scotland, and Australia. I like travelling.

My Sister's Wedding

In 2017, my sister and Chris got married. It was a very exciting time for them, as well as for our families and for me. Kaila and Chris were together for a long time, around eleven or twelve years, before they got engaged. That was OK with our families because we knew they would be together for a long time, technically forever.

I was excited when Kaila and Chris got engaged. They used FaceTime to call us and show us the ring, and I got the privilege of seeing the ring first, even though I couldn't really see it and I didn't know if it was the left or right hand, but she was waving her hand a lot and looked happy. My sister and Chris made sure that I was part of the wedding as much as I could be, like food tastings and seeing the venues. Kaila asked me to do a blessing at the wedding and that was pretty cool. I also wanted to usher people to their seats before the ceremony so I could say hi to everyone.

The wedding was held at the Royal Botanical Gardens in Burlington. It was real nice there. About ninety-nine to one hundred people came, and obviously our families were there. Some of Kaila's and Chris' work colleagues were there, and they were very friendly. They were "huggers." We did our family pictures and had dinner and all that wedding stuff, and then came time for the blessing. I was a little nervous, but all I had to do was say, "Thank you for the food in front of us, the family and friends with us, and the joy around us." And then for a joke I said, "Rub-a-dub-dub, thanks for the grub."

After that we just had a good time. We danced and enjoyed the company. It was a very good experience, and I would not have had it any other way. I was glad to be a part of it as much as I could be, because my sister does so much for me, as you can probably tell. I'm very happy to do things for her when I have the opportunity. I try to pay her back a little bit to thank her for everything she does for me on a daily basis.

One of my first public speaking engagements, where I reminded people of my dad.

My sister's wedding with my family.

Having fun working in groups at Re:Action4Inclusion.

At Sobeys using my height to my advantage.

My Special Olympics team. We are called the Welland Warriors.

My very first tattoo in Burlington, just after I had a doughnut, what a day!

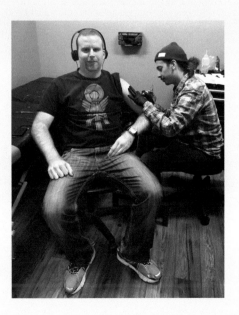

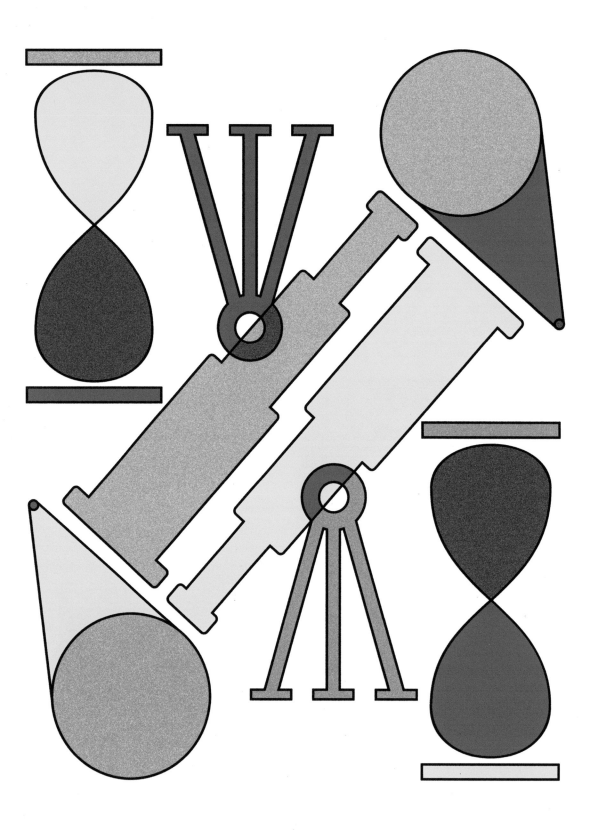

10

ILLUSTRATION BY CHRIS LYNN

The Future

So... what's next?

I am not too sure about the answer to that question, but I am willing to try anything. There's a possibility that I might one day go to college, but we'll have to see about that. Maybe by then I will have a girlfriend—but I have to find somebody first! I would like to have a full time job at Sobeys and continue my public speaking. I'm always looking for new and exciting opportunities, and of course I want to continue to advocate for individuals with disabilities.

I would like to thank everybody who helped me with writing my book, and also I would like to thank you for reading it. I hope you enjoyed it. I also hope that reading my book has helped you to not just see me as a person with a disability; I hope that you will see me as someone who is deserving of the same opportunities in life as those without disabilities. My book is meant to inspire anybody who has been told they can't do something.

All my life I wanted to read a book by myself with no help, but now I think I've achieved something even cooler: now I'm an author with a book of my own. My friend pointed out to me that no one makes a book all by themselves; even famous authors need help writing and designing and publishing. I can't read or write, but I got the help I needed, and now you're holding my book in your hands. It just goes to show that anything is possible. Focus on your strengths and find ways to make it happen.

I'll leave you with this: if you want to do something, you should do it. And as Ellen Degeneres would say: be kind to one another.

Bye!
Michael

About the Author

Michael is a young adult who lives and works in the Niagara Region of Ontario, Canada. He is a determined, compassionate, and talented individual who has written his first book. Michael has autism and an intellectual disability and is a passionate public speaker. He has presented to students at the secondary, college, and university levels, as well parents and teachers, about the importance of belonging and inclusion. He sits on the board of Community Living Ontario, through which he advocates for individuals like himself. Michael hopes to write many more books and continue to make an impact in the world through his stories.